Mission Trip Spanish

Contents

Introduction: What is Mission Trip Spanish?

Mission Trip Spanish is designed to raise your level of Spanish quickly, allowing you to speak, listen, and understand the people you encounter in Latin American countries.

When people go on mission trips to Spanish-speaking countries, they almost always say one thing when they return: "I wish I had learned more Spanish before going. I had a hard time communicating with people, even though I wanted to." This is despite the fact that most people in the United States have taken Spanish classes at some point, whether in elementary or middle school, high school or college. You may have taken three or more years of Spanish in school, and should have the confidence to say whatever you like while on your mission trip. However, most former Spanish students cannot string along a coherent thought while south of the border, and the people they are serving get confused when they speak the language.

This can be frustrating. I know, because it was the experience of myself and those around me on my first mission trip. On my first trip, I went to Mexico for two weeks after graduating from high school, where I had aced my Spanish classes. When I arrived, however, I had a hard time recalling basic, everyday phrases. Worst of all, some of the common terms I needed I had never been taught. After all the classes and studying, I couldn't even say, "Nice to meet you," or "Thank you for your hospitality." It's a rough feeling when you were never taught the Spanish that might have deepened your relationship with those you serve and opened up new doors on your mission trip.

But I don't accept defeat easily. It was after this that I invested in the research, trials, errors and successes it took to come up with the Mission Trip Spanish solution. To be able to offer you Mission Trip Spanish, I had to become a master at learning the language, myself. By studying language experts[1], taking specialized Spanish courses, traveling to Latin American countries and studying a variety of second language learning[2] systems, I ultimately created a one of my own --a system tailored specifically for the mission trip. Once refined, I used it myself, under a five week experiment, to see if I could successfully interpret colloquial Spanish in an official capacity. Success!

Mission Trip Spanish helps you communicate and connect with the people of your destination country. The method is easy, concise and effective. You will finally be able to relate to people, to say what you want to say, and ultimately, to get the most out of your mission trip. That is my dream for you, and I'm committed to help make it your reality.

Important Notes About This Book

1. Unless you are a long-term Spanish student, you will **not** become fully fluent in the language after this five week course --and that's okay!
2. You **will** be able to communicate easily with those you serve. This is the goal.
3. You **will** need a basic knowledge of the language. If you've taken one or two Spanish classes, this book will be what you need to grow to a conversational level.
4. **Nobody expects** you sound like a native. Fluent speakers who live immersed in the language for many years struggle themselves to achieve a perfect accent[3]. Native Spanish speakers are forgiving. It is enough to be understood.
5. That said, we will focus here on getting you to **highest level possible in the shortest amount of time**, so that you will be ready for your mission trip.

How to Use This Book

This is not a classic text book. You won't master one chapter during one week, then move on to the next the following week, never looking back until test time. You only have five weeks to practice the methods in this book and start running with the language. So master one concept per day during the first week. From there you can pretty much pick what you'd like to work on daily, until you are ready to get on the plane. It might be hectic, but it is also fun and very worth it in the end. Your test will be the most exciting exam you've taken in your life: talking, communicating, laughing and maybe even crying with the human beings you're going to serve during your weeks in a foreign country.

Here are the five elements that make up the Mission Trip Spanish learning method. Again, be prepared to digest one a day during the first week of reading this book, and also continue practicing each element as soon as you learn it. Using the method outlined here, and people/resources from your destination country (yes, that's right), you will:

1. Speak Spanish with a native speaker
2. Read short, interesting articles
3. Watch movies and
4. Listen to music from your destination country
5. Easily memorize words and phrases from a personalized list that you, yourself, will compile.

Experienced mission trip volunteers, language students and others who have experienced the challenges of learning Spanish for their mission trips have also experienced great success by implementing the tips, tricks, and solid step-by-step instructions found in Mission Trip Spanish.

Paul, a student from Georgia, says:
"I've been on mission trips in Guatemala, Bolivia and now Argentina. I can honestly say that this method has made my latest mission trip a thousand times more memorable."

Sierra from Asheville, North Carolina agrees:
"Let me start off by saying that using this method has been one of the best educational experiences of my life. When I started, I honestly had no idea how much Spanish I would learn. When I got to Mexico, I could not believe how much I had accomplished."

Alex of White Sands, New Mexico, talks about his trip to Guatemala:
"I had so much fun in Guatemala, thanks to Mission Trip Spanish! I followed all the steps and even got myself a language partner before I left. I definitely intend to continue with Spanish after this. The fire is lit. Thanks!"

If you follow Mission Trip Spanish, you should learn and retain, in a very short time, exactly what you need to know for your mission trip to Latin America, AND you should get twice as much personal enjoyment out of your mission trip. Using real, spoken Spanish helps you stand out from the crowd and avoid all of the miscommunication and confusion you might otherwise have experienced.

Mission Spanish Trip invites you to be the kind of person other people want to emulate: the kind of person who takes action and does so with a purpose. Be the kind of person at whom other people marvel saying, "I have no idea how John/Joan learned Spanish so quickly!"

Mission Trip Spanish is powerful and will allow you to speak Spanish with native speakers from Latin America almost immediately, right here, right now. Each chapter of this book will get you closer to your goal of being able to speak with those you will serve using Spanish that is useful --not the Spanish you learned in school that causes native speakers to look at you funny[4]. As you read through this book, you will quickly develop the ability to speak Spanish as it is currently spoken.

You will take control of your Spanish learning. By following this book, the next five weeks (or less) will transform your Spanish. This is the exact method that I used to become an interpreter for a government agency and the exact method that I continue to use to become even better at what I do. This is not your high school Spanish class. This is not verb conjugation charts or crossword puzzles. This is a method that you can follow step-by-step in order to speak and understand Spanish while on your mission trip and beyond. These steps are powerful, but only if you apply them every single day for the next five weeks, while you prepare your heart and mind for service in Latin America.

Let's get started.

Your friend,

Tyler
Mission Trip Spanish

P.S. Sign up here for the Mission Trip Spanish email list. You'll get free content designed to complement this book while you are on your Spanish learning journey. Visit: www.MissionTripSpanish.com/contact

Chapter 1: Learn Spanish, No Super Brain Necessary

When I was in high school, I was friends with students who were considered to be very "gifted" in their ability to study very little and to perform very well on exams and tests. In fact, some of these "gifted" folks were believed to have photographic memories. This ability seemed to be present in all subjects throughout our time in school, including in Spanish class. These students would study very little (if at all) and get straight A's on all of their exams and projects.

For the longest time, I marveled at their ability to memorize very well and recall things that took me a long time to study. I continued to marvel at their abilities up until I went to college. It was then that I saw these straight-A no-study types fall like flies when it came to their ability to absorb and retain huge amounts of information. This was especially true in Spanish courses. It seemed like they had it all together for a little while, but they lacked the foresight or the necessary knowledge to carry their abilities any further than a few days.

If you have been studying Spanish for any length of time, you know that it is NOT about being naturally talented. In fact, the ability to learn any language does not exclusively depend on your natural talent.

In high school, I was not considered to be one of these highly "gifted" folks, but as someone who could focus on what I believed to be important (such as the underlying causes of success). I developed habits that practically forced my own success. I excelled in areas that I knew would be useful to me later in life. For example, I would sign up for activities such as extemporaneous speaking on global affairs and theatre classes. Both are forms of public speaking, a skill that is downright frightening for most people to put into practice, even though it is necessary in both the public and private sectors.

When I got to college, I focused on laying a foundation for learning that would be unbreakable. I developed methods that could override the "gifted" folks and that could push me to another level. I soon perfected my methods of memorization and learning, graduating early from both college and graduate school. I became a self-made, straight-A student in graduate school, publishing my first academic journal article, serving as the president of a student association, earning accolades such as the "Who's Who Among College and University Students" and other awards, as well as presenting at many research conferences and working as a graduate assistant for a leadership program... all this while re-teaching myself Spanish.

Why am I telling you all this? When I re-taught myself Spanish, I was a very busy person! I know you are also busy, but Mission Trip Spanish is definitely worth the few minutes you put towards it per day, because this method can help you get amazing results.

Below, and in the next chapter also, are a few tips to keep in mind that will help maximize your experience with Mission Trip Spanish.

Learning Tip #1: Just Imagine How It Will Feel to Communicate in Spanish

In order to succeed in learning Spanish for your mission trip, you will need to think about the outcome. Think about how great it will feel to be able to speak to those you are serving, to understand them, to connect with them on a personal level.

I know that the first time I realized that I was actually able to connect with someone in Spanish, I felt overwhelmed. I could feel myself thinking in Spanish, understanding what was being said to me, and adding my own ideas and input into the conversation.

Think of your reasons for learning. Mission Trip Spanish is here to show you how you can get to a high level of Spanish very quickly, and if you want, this book will show you how to maintain the two languages so that you can truly live in two cultures.

This book is your resource, but before you can use this resource well, you've got to keep in mind your reasons for using it in the first place! Think about why you want to learn Spanish. You already know that one great reason is so that you can communicate with those you serve while on your mission trip. I challenge you to find other reasons, small reasons, that add up to making your Spanish learning a lot more enjoyable.

When I first started re-learning Spanish, I found that simply going through a workbook or listening to an audio tape was not very fun or motivating. It was then that I started to branch out and develop a method based on what people enjoy and NOT on willpower. (Learn more about willpower versus motivation in Chapter 7.) When you do things in Spanish that you enjoy, rather than focusing on the willpower necessary to go through dull workbooks and verb conjugation charts, you will see a dramatic difference in your learning.

My Spanish-speaking friends and their families were the most shocked when I told them how long I had been using my new method. On one occasion, I was at an old friend's house. His parents only speak Spanish, and they recently had a cousin move in who was also monolingual. Before using my method, I would just smile, nod, and say some of the few words that I knew, in order to be courteous. When I arrived at their house, this time, everyone assumed that things would go similarly to the last time we had seen each other. To everyone's amazement (including mine!) I found myself effortlessly understanding my friend's family, and they, in turn, were understanding me! I could not believe that my Spanish learning had created a situation where I could speak and connect with others who I had previously only known through nods and smiles.

After I started developing Mission Trip Spanish, I noticed that my friends began asking how I was able to accomplish so much in such a short time. Some began asking me what my memorization techniques were so that they could apply them to learning other languages. I was happy to share my experiences, and curious to see if others would get the same fulfillment and enjoyment out of using a method that is focused on fun and motivation, rather than dullness and repetition. I was even happier when a friend of mine, who had decided to learn Italian after going on a trip to Italy with her church, asked me about my method. After laying out the method for her and showing her how fun the process of learning another language can be, she assured me that she would give it a try. A couple of months passed before I heard from my friend again. When I did, I was excited to hear that she had taken my advice to heart. She shared her progress with me. She told me about her experiences connecting with Italians, having friendships in another language, and her newfound ability to enjoy another culture while learning the language.

This is why I do what I do. I am motivated by the transformation my friends have gone through when they learn another language through the Mission Trip Spanish method. I also love the personal impact I am able to have on those around me by my being able to communicate in Spanish. These are just a few stories about how this method has changed my life and the lives of my friends and fellow Christians.

Those whom I have helped learn Spanish for their mission trip have given me motivation to keep sharing my method--hence, this book. I promise that once you have read it, you will see how easy it really is to become proficient in Spanish for your mission trip. Using motivation and fun in your learning will trump willpower every time. Choosing to learn by speaking with real people and using real material rather than an outdated one-size-fits-all workbook can help skyrocket your ability to connect with real people while on your mission trip and beyond.

Chapter 2: Light Your Desire to Speak!

In virtually every set of steps you encounter in life, the first step is considered to be of special significance. This chapter is about that first step: kindling the desire to communicate effectively in a foreign language.

In order to speak Spanish in a way that is powerful, in a way that is meaningful, while you are on your mission trip, you must light a fire inside yourself that goes beyond the clichés of "Where's the bathroom?" and "*Hay un gato en mis pantalones*" (although both phrases will serve you well if you ever have the occasion to use them). Before all else, you must light the fire within yourself to go and serve your fellow people, people who are fun, people who are happy, people who would most certainly help you in your time of need, given different circumstances, just as you are there to help them. Prepare yourself to meet intelligent people who share your desire to communicate and who share your desire to help build the Kingdom of God on Earth.

The most important thing to consider when you start your journey towards speaking Spanish in preparation for your mission trip is connecting with the people that you will be serving. People. That is what they are. The people that you will serve have goals, dreams, aspirations, fears, smiles, tears and joys. They share many of the same deep-seated wants and desires that you and I have. They care deeply for their parents, for their church and for their friends.

As a young child visiting my grandparents and uncle in Texas, near the border with Mexico, I created images in my head from what I had heard the adults around me say about Mexico, about the people that live there, and about the dangers associated with traveling to places that spoke Spanish. One day while riding in a pickup truck from San Benito to McAllen with my uncle, I was glued to the window. My uncle asked me why I was scanning the bland desert landscape so intently. I told him that I wanted to catch a glimpse of one of those immigrants I had heard so much about on the news and from the other adults around me, so that I could see for myself what they really looked like. His response to the seven-year-old version of Tyler stayed with me into adulthood and sparked in me a lifelong interest in the people of Latin America and a desire to help those who seek to improve their lot in life. My uncle said the following truism: "They're just people."

Suddenly all of my previous images conjured up by the talking heads on the news, the opinions of the adults in my life, and the misconceptions that I had been fed through my culture's ethnocentric eye were called into question by the simple analysis of my uncle that these people were, indeed, people. Just like me. And suddenly, it became fascinating to see what could be learned from these people who are not to be feared or to be hated. But how could I do that? I did not speak Spanish, and nobody I knew spoke Spanish to any degree. Thus the mystery of what was being said during the Spanish services and events at church, the news stories being covered on Univision, and the events that were taking place around the world that were not covered on my English-speaking news channels became absolutely fascinating. I wanted to hear about these Spanish-speaking people in their own language, and perhaps become a more informed American citizen in the process.

This was my fire: my desire to understand and interact with the culture and language of a people. Perhaps this narration has lit your own fire to help people, while also respecting them.

Now let's put you ahead of the pack and on your way to having the most rewarding mission trip to Latin America of your life.

Learning Tip #2 Make the Internet Your New Best Friend
Think about your best friend and all the things that you appreciate about your best friend. Certainly, their personality plays a big role. Then there are the experiences you have shared together, and perhaps even some shared beliefs or ways of looking at things.

What if I told you that you could develop a connection with someone much like your best friend, but with the added benefit of them speaking the exact same version of Spanish that comes from the same country you are traveling to for your mission trip? Imagine the things you could learn about the country and its people before you even arrive. Imagine now that your best friend, without judgement and without stress, explains things about the country you will be traveling to and teaches you things about the language and culture well before you step on the plane. How cool would that be? You would already be able to connect with the people you meet by sharing with them the things that you have learned from your friend!

Sounds crazy, right? How can you do this? Well, I'll tell you what you probably already know: the internet is the key to finding your new, Spanish-speaking, best friend.

Learning Tip #3: Speak Spanish Regularly with a Native Speaker from Your Destination Country
Now, I know that you may be thinking about the horror stories of grandmas and grandpas being scammed by foreign princes who persuaded them to send off their money in hopes of receiving a big return, and how you've got to be careful while communicating with people online. Learning Spanish is not some get-rich-quick scheme, but if you are a youth and require your parents' permission to go online to learn Spanish from actual Spanish-speakers, then just have one of them sit with you during the sessions to find out just how harmless this method is.

I cannot stress enough the importance of speaking with actual people very frequently in preparation for speaking Spanish while on your mission trip. Above all else, getting a feel for how people talk, what words and phrases are used most often, and what words are unique to the country where you will be traveling is of great importance. When you start your journey towards speaking Spanish for your mission trip, you must make speaking Spanish with an actual native speaker an absolute priority. If you find that you are unable to do anything else in this book due to time constraints, do this. You will find that this one powerful rule will make your ability to speak and understand Spanish skyrocket in comparison with those who simply bought some software in preparation for the trip. I MEAN IT! Unless you are an absolute beginner, using software will only get in your way, take up your time, and slow your progress.

In a later chapter, I will tell you exactly which websites I use and how I use them to continue improving my abilities in Spanish. For now, just know that the importance of speaking daily with actual native speakers from the country where you are going to be traveling is of great importance.

Why is speaking so important? When you speak to people, you can begin to understand the rhythm of the way that natives of that country speak. You learn the most common phrases that are unique to that country's dialect, and you learn about words and phrases that have one specific meaning in that particular country while the same words and phrases may mean something entirely different in another. For example: have you ever tried to say a word that you learned in Spanish class to a native speaker, and the native speaker looks at you puzzled or says, "I don't know what you're trying to say." It is frustrating right? Well, many times, this comes from the fact that what is often taught in Spanish class in school does not translate into practical usage when you go to a country where the language is actually spoken. Learning phrases like *"vuestra merced"* from Don Quixote, for example, may not get you very far in a Nicaraguan eatery. Thus, learning what people say and how they say it in the country where you will be going on your mission trip is incredibly important.

Keep all of this in mind over the next five weeks and you should have such a rewarding feeling when you are able to have meaningful conversations with the people you serve while on your mission trip in Latin America. "How can you be so sure," you say? Because you will already have had deep and rewarding conversations with people every day for five weeks before you even step foot in the country! This is worth it.

Later on, I will teach you how to find the right person or persons with whom you can speak in Spanish every single day over the next five weeks. Just keep reading, learning, and soaking up the techniques I am showing you here. Once you land in the country, you might feel like an NBA player who has been warming up all pre-season, ready to use what he has learned, and prepared to have fun with it, too.

Chapter 3: Apps and Websites- Making Your Learning Stress-Free and Efficient

Once you have determined that you are going to get serious about learning the Spanish you'll need for your mission trip, you'll need some tools that are simple and straightforward, and that don't waste your time. I am going to show you the exact applications and websites that are used by multilinguals, polyglots, and language-learning experts when they need to tackle a language in a short amount of time. These tools are meant to help you on your path to successfully speaking and understanding people on your Spanish-speaking journey. You may think that what I am about to suggest is a product that comes in a box, can be bought at the airport, or is receiving a special endorsement. None of this is true, because experts who learn languages quickly and with a purpose NEVER waste their time on such heavily marketed products. Instead, the tools I use, and what you are about to use, don't cost a thing.

I speak from experience when I say that every single one of the people whom I have met that have used expensive software --let alone the cheap variety- and insisted that it "works" cannot hold a conversation about any topic. In short, they wasted their money. Wouldn't it be better to spend all those hundreds of dollars on something more worthwhile --your mission trip, for instance? But enough preaching to the choir! Let's get you set up with all the tools you need.

Tools: Apps, Apps and More Apps

On my phone, at this very moment, there are a number of applications that get plenty of use throughout the week, and sometimes throughout the day. These diamonds include WordReference, Reverso Context, TuneIn Radio, WhatsApp, and the application for my favorite newspaper in Spanish where I get nearly all of my articles (more on this later). If you were to attend conferences, listen to seminars, or purchase courses taught by the greatest language-learning minds of our time, almost every one of these tools would be mentioned as being the keys[5] to language-learning today. There are some tools that I have not included in my language-learning repertoire, but that many people find crucial to their success. Among these include the Anki Flashcard software. I believe that the concept and functionality of this tool is likely to be very useful, but I already use a tried and true method of language-learning. Mission Trip Spanish doesn't need paid apps.

Here's more information on what we do use:

App #1: WordReference
This is one of the best applications that you will ever see. It doesn't cost a thing, and is used all over the world by language experts when they are learning a new language. It can be used for Spanish, French, Chinese, you name it! This tool is by far one of the most important you will have as you begin this journey. It will often give you the pronunciation of the words you look up, along with context. Context is key to language-learning. If you do not understand the context, you will get lost, and when you get lost, you'll get frustrated. WordReference is your saving grace when it comes to learning new words and phrases.

Are you watching a movie and want to know what a particular word is? Start typing it in and WordReference will start giving you options to choose from. When you've picked an option, it will give you a sentence that uses the word or phrase in context, so you know how it is used in spoken language. I cannot stress enough how crucial this application will be as you prepare for your mission trip.

App #2: Reverso Context
This application is also a well-known application. Be careful, though. Much of this site is generated from users, and is therefore more colloquial than WordReference. It does have its merits, however, especially if you have run across slang or colloquial words and phrases that you cannot seem to find in WordReference. In this regard, Reverso Context almost always has you covered.

App #3: TuneIn Radio

Use this application as much as humanly possible before your trip. This is such an easy win, when it comes to getting prepared for your mission trip. Think of the country that you are about to visit. Do you think that the area where you are going to serve has plenty of television, plenty of luxuries, and plenty of magazines? The chances are good that this is not the case. But radio. Radio is everywhere and in every household. Grandmothers all over Latin America are eating toast and drinking coffee in the morning while listening to the local radio station. Now you can be like those grandmothers! But seriously, regardless of age, in virtually every Latin American country, the radio is one of the primary means of media and entertainment on a country-wide scale. Why not tap into this?

Do you think that your ability to listen to and understand native speakers from your destination country would be improved if you listen to those native speakers in their own dialect for five whole weeks, before you arrive? Well, you are right. Your ability will be leaps and bounds about what you would expect, and certainly leaps and bounds above those who are using boxed software to learn a plain vanilla version of the language that is never spoken where you are going. Therefore, the best thing to do at this point is to add the TuneIn Radio app to your phone (or create a link on your desktop) and start using this tool. This tool will be there when you are eating breakfast, coming home from school or work, and in the shower (if you have a waterproof case). "But how do I find the right radio station?" you might be asking. Well, you have two solid options. You can refer to the people who you talk to on a regular basis from that country (more on this later), or you can just do what I did. Go to your favorite search engine, type in "most popular radio stations in [insert country here]" and see what the statistics are. For me, I listen to Radio Mitre all of the time, but that is because I have a reason to. I married into a family of Argentines. Thus I listen to Mitre, speak Rioplatense, drink yerba mate, and cheer for Boca. However, when I go on mission trips I ALWAYS change my strategy in preparation for the trip. I shift from Argentine media outlets to media outlets and channels from the country I am about to visit. I suggest that you do the same. If you love the idea of speaking like a Spaniard, but are going to help people on a mission trip to Guatemala, learn about how things are said in Guatemala over the next five weeks, instead.

Be prepared to NOT understand much at first. This is okay and is to be expected. When you first start listening to radio in Spanish, you may understand hardly anything for the first two weeks! The people on the radio are not talking fast (unless it is a soccer announcer), but your ears will simply not be used to hearing all the different sounds. It will seem like an uninterrupted block of sounds at first, but after a few weeks, you will be able to distinguish individual words, and even sense the patterns and meanings of certain phrases.

Everyone goes through a phase of language-learning in which the pace of understanding seems slow. But think of the beauty that it is! It isn't slow at all --especially compared to your rate of learning in Spanish class. In fact, your brain is rapidly adapting to the foreign language it is hearing. Our brains are made for language; the Good Lord made us so! Even those who are older and who think that they are not good at learning languages because of their age will not be able to say that if they put in the time to just listen to the radio. You will thank me for this once you've arrived in the country and realized that you've been listening to people speaking in the exact same dialect, rhythm, and tone for the past five weeks!

App #4: Skype
The phone application version of Skype is very useful when you are trying to find out if your pals are online and whether they have time to chat, but imagine how much it would cost to have a few Skype conversations when connected using your data plan! Therefore, make sure you are only connected via Wifi when using Skype, or you can just stick to the computer version to avoid mishaps. Top language experts recommend spending at least an hour per day speaking a foreign language in preparation for a trip to a foreign country. Using Skype greatly improves your ability to reach that goal. I'll tell you more about the nugget of gold that is Skype for your computer in just a bit.

App #5: Whatsapp
Take it from me. My language partner and I, even if we have not spoken on Skype for a while, ALWAYS talk on Whatsapp. Whatsapp is an

application for your phone that allows you to text, call, or send voice messages to other Whatsapp users for free. That's right. If your family's wireless bill is through the roof because of texts and calls, consider Whatsapp. BUT also consider it for your language-learning. From my point of view, this application is almost as crucial to your language-learning as WordReference or Skype.

Tools: Websites

The internet is a wonderful thing. You are able to get everything that you could possibly need with a few clicks. Language-learning is much more accessible than a decade ago. But HOW to use the internet to learn Spanish in a short amount of time for your mission trip is another matter entirely. In fact, that's how this book got started. I saw a need for information about learning Spanish for mission trips to Latin America and I knew that I could help my friends and fellow Christians to reach their goals. I feel sad every single time that I talk to someone who has just come back from their mission trip to Latin America and says: "I just wish that I would have known more Spanish so that I could talk to the people we were serving." It saddens me because I know I could have helped! There are so many resources out there, so many that it is easy to get overwhelmed by them and to just give up. Don't do that just yet!

There are some resources that you can start using right now that will bypass all of the so-called helpful material about language-learning, so you can start learning exactly what you need to know for your mission trip. I will tell you about the ones that work and how to use them.

Language-learning is meant to be a fun process. Too often, people get stuck learning in a way that is boring, monotonous, and most tragically, ineffective at helping you to actually learn the Spanish you need. Let me show you just how easy it is to get yourself motivated and ready to start tackling the Spanish you want to learn using internet resources, web pages, in particular.

Site #1: Italki.com
This is the most epic site there is in language-learning. It's how I met my language partner, how I keep meeting new language partners as my destination country changes, and how I am able to get my speaking

practice in with native speakers from those countries, even when I live on the opposite side of the planet.

How It Works: Getting the Best from Italki.com

Just log on, make your account, and start looking for tutors from the country where you are going to do mission trip work. If you do not want to pay for tutoring, you can also meet fellow language learners that want to learn your language. Most often, you will exchange Skype information, and voila! You are now able to connect with people from around the world who speak the exact dialect of the country that you will visit, instantly! You will soon realize the power of being able to connect with native Spanish speakers who want to help you learn their language. This is one of the most amazing tools of modern language-learning.

Gone are the days of the pen pal. You can now connect with live people from your destination country and ask them all the questions you have wanted to ask. "But I don't have any questions" you might say. Well, guess what? I've got a solution for you. Take a moment to bookmark this page then go take a look at the chapter with phrases for mission trips towards the end of this book. These are all phrases that you will likely find the occasion to use when you are on your mission trip. Now think for a moment, what is something that you have always wanted to say in Spanish. What is a phrase that you think you might need while you are away on your mission trip?

Let's say that you need to go to the bathroom, but there's no toilet paper and the toilet is clogged (the struggle is real). Can you think of how you would say that in Spanish? For most people, "*Donde está el baño*" is the only phrase that comes to mind immediately. But uh-oh, you already found the *baño*... what now? Well, now would be a good time to think back to the time when you asked your Spanish tutor from Italki about how to say that phrase in Spanish. Boom. Problem (crisis) solved. Are you beginning to see the benefit of preparing early?

I want you to take a moment, right now, and write a list of ten things that you would like to know how to say. Write them all out and don't worry about trying to translate them yourself (chances are that you will get it wrong, and that's ok). You must set up a tutoring time with your language partner and have that list ready. During your first session, you'll notice that your language partner will say something like, "What would you like to know?" BAM, hit him with your first phrase! From there, she or he will think about it and tell you what they would say. You can even ask them if they can type it out for you. From there, the conversation might turn to something related, and you will begin to learn new words and phrases that you didn't even anticipate! You can ask your new pal about music that they would recommend for you to listen to, and they might even offer to help you translate the lyrics. The possibilities are endless once you have a language partner that cares about your learning, one with whom you truly connect.

Over the next five weeks, try to have as many sessions with your language partner as possible. You will find that your conversations will become more complex, and you will be able to learn even more about the words and phrases that you would like to know once you arrive in the country. By the time your five weeks are up, you will feel like you have been living the language and the culture for over a month before you even arrived. What an amazing feeling. Seriously, there is nothing like it.

Now, remember how I said that you'll likely be talking to your language partner over Skype? Well now would be a good time to get a Skype account if you don't already have one. For privacy's sake, use your common sense when filling out the information needed for Skype (or consult your parents if you are underage). Skype is a very safe method of communication, but if you are like me, you want to be careful whenever you go online. So go ahead and make your account, and get it set up on your computer; get the app for your phone, and you are good to go. Many language-learning experts agree that Skype is the absolute must-have tool when learning languages. At the beginning of almost every single meeting with a new language partner on Italki (or any language-learning site) the request for your Skype name comes within the first five sentences. So get familiar with how Skype works and get yourself a microphone, because you will be using it a lot!

Site #2: Dropbox
Why do I mention a website tool that has nothing to do with languages? Because it has everything to do with languages. As you begin learning, you

will find that you have plenty of phrases that you wish you knew in Spanish, but you have nowhere to store this information. This is where Dropbox comes in.

How It Works: Storing Master Lists on Dropbox

Open a new word processing document. Make two columns, then fill the left side of the page with English words and phrases you would like to know. Leave the right side blank. As you meet with your language partner, ask how you would say those phrases or words. Once you have finished talking to your language partner, take a minute to add the Spanish version of those phrases to your document. Remember, you can always ask your language partner to spell everything out using the chat box as the conversation progresses. Save the new document to your Dropbox, and you are ready to go! You have just created your first master list for Spanish, and if you've downloaded the app to your phone, you can access it anywhere!

Now that you have this master list, you can continue to add to it as you find new words and phrases that you would like to learn. The magic in this comes when you are out in the real world and you hear people using the terms and phrases that you had already committed to memory weeks ago! Trust me, you will be glad that you used Dropbox to save your files. The more phrases and words you add to your master list, the more valuable it will become to you. So take heart, write things down and back up your work.

Site #3: YouTube.com

What I am about to tell you may not be apparently obvious, but it will make sense once you think about it for a moment. Here it is: People around the world are living their lives, entertaining themselves, talking to people, watching movies and watching YouTubers, who are providing entertaining content right this very second on a site that is free to access. Let that sink in for a moment.

Now consider this. There are likely Spanish channels on YouTube.com that are specific to the country where you will be traveling On those channels, people from that country are watching things that they find funny, hilarious, entertaining, interesting, you name it! And chances are, you will find them funny, entertaining, and interesting as well. So what's a language learner to do? Well, I am here to show you. Just log onto YouTube, and start finding some content that you really enjoy, from the country you are going to visit. For me, I LOVE watching YouTubers. They are hilarious, they speak from the heart, and they speak like normal people. In other words, they talk like normal people who are using the language to communicate. They are not like your high school Spanish teacher who wants to show you the Don Quixote movie and make you look at a Frida Kahlo painting.

Don't get me wrong, people from Spanish-speaking countries had to learn about classics too, but the classics are just not important when you have only five weeks to learn everything you need to know for your mission trip! Instead, the most important part of speaking Spanish, for our purposes, is just that: speaking and communicating with your fellow humans. Remember my uncle's wise words, "They are just people."

Personally, I use YouTube.com for four main reasons:

1.   For good, clean entertainment from hilarious YouTubers in Spanish
2.   For watching movies from the country that I am interested in, for free
3.   For finding catchy songs from the country that I am interested in
4.   For keeping on top of new language-learning techniques as they come out

I suggest that you do the same thing. Go to YouTube.com and start searching.

Chapter 4: You Can Read Short, Interesting Material and Gain Maximum Results

Many people believe that simply going to a country and being immersed in the language should be enough to learn Spanish. Well, if one was in that country for a year, this could be somewhat true. However, being in the country for a week or two is not necessarily going to give you all the tools you need to be able to express yourself in the way that you would like.

From speaking with native speakers and being around them frequently, you certainly will learn a great deal. And just as in English, you can tell if a person is well read, or has a firm grasp on the language. Such a person often has a wider view of the world and has learned about a variety of topics through reading. This is apparent in the way they speak, the words they use and the understanding they express, when speaking about subjects that you may not have had much exposure to. This is exactly the same in Spanish. In the country you are visiting, there are professors, there are doctors, there are students studying what you study, and there are very smart people who work in professions similar to yours and who produce reading material you would find interesting . Thus, if you look for it, you will find reading material that interests you, with the added benefit that it is in Spanish!

If you want to improve your abilities in Spanish to a point where you can speak about a wide range of topics, have a better understanding of the people with whom you interact and connect with people who use similar words and patterns of speech as yourself, you need to read in Spanish. You need to read in Spanish, and you need to do so consistently. Then you will automatically begin to realize that the real-world Spanish you are learning is far from what you learned in high school Spanish class, and is a lot more interesting!

If you follow this advice, you can learn Spanish, while reading about things that you actually care about (although there is nothing wrong with Don Quixote). Mission Trip Spanish is not a dull workbook that you will try for 15 minutes and then wonder why you bought it in the first place. This is a method that works.

So why articles?[6] Why not books? Many people believe the advice for novice readers is to find their favorite vampire book and get the Spanish version so that they can compare what they read with the English version and have a great time pulling out their fingernails. This does not work! Think about it. You have limited time in the day, a limited attention span that comes with a busy lifestyle and a limited budget that may not include buying multiple versions of a popular book.

That aside, when you are just starting out, a full novel is not something that will give you the results you are looking for. You are about to go on a mission trip to a Latin American country, not to a book club. The words, phrases, and topics that you learn about in your favorite English book that has been translated into Spanish will not help you when you go. You will only get frustrated.

Instead of all taking such a hit to your morale, I suggest doing something that will keep your interest, that will be brief, and that will be a powerful tool to prepare you for your journey. It should also be fun. Where can you find this? Online. For free. That's right! Online newspaper articles: They can be accessed from any place in the world. Reading articles will immediately provide you with interesting material in a condensed format that's written by educated professionals in the language that you are learning. The topics will also be current and relevant to your destination country!

How It Works for Maximum Results

Now that you know about the merits of using articles over books or other reading material in Spanish, where do you find these articles in the first place?

Step #1 to Reading for Results: Search
Go to your favorite online search engine, and type in "Newspapers from [insert country]." Then look for a link that will provide you with a list of the newspapers from that country. From there, you can look up which are the most popular in the country you will be visiting. Decide which you would like to read, then begin scanning its website for a topic that interests you. You may be interested in politics, world events, food columns, or traffic jams. Whatever interests you at the time, look for it on their website and do not stop looking until you have found something that:

1. Has really caught your eye,
2. Contains words that you have never heard of
3. Contains words that have to do with a topic that you would like to speak about in conversation, and
4. Is just long enough to fill 1 ½ to 2 pages worth of printed material.

Step #2 to Reading for Results: Print
Once you have made your selection, make sure to print out the article

(preferably in color, if there are images), and staple the pages. Now you have your very own reading material about something that's fascinating, fun and free. The best part, of course, is that it's from the country you will be visiting.

Step #3 to Reading for Results: Say It Aloud
Now that you have this piece of pure gold in your hand, I will show you how to make sure to use it properly. Start by reading the article out loud. Try to make sure that you are speaking in a Spanish accent, then move on to Step #4.

Step #4 to Reading for Results: Underline Unfamiliar Words
When you come to a word that you do not know, underline it. You should be underlining frequently. Often times you may think that you can glean the significance of a phrase or word because of its similarity to an English word, but a good deal of the time you would be wrong! So if you have not committed a word to memory, just underline it. When you go back to translate it, the actual significance of the word may surprise you.

Step #5 to Reading for Results: Pause
After reading through the article out loud and making the underlines, you may feel that you have a difficult challenge ahead of you. Nothing could be further from the truth. In fact, this method is powerfully simple and easy. You may be looking at your article and seeing pages that are full of underlines and words that you cannot pronounce. It's all in how you look at it. Instead you should see a couple of pages of authentic Spanish that you are about to totally master!

Step #6 to Reading for Results: Translate Unfamiliar Words
To make this work for you, begin by looking up the significance of each word and phrase you do not know. The easiest way to do this is to download two free apps mentioned above, WordReference and Reverso, if you have not already done so. You will find that between these two applications, you will be able to accurately translate the words and phrases you do not know in a very short amount of time. You may also use the website versions of these two apps in order to find the answers you are looking for. As you look up the words and phrases that you have underlined, draw a line from the underlined word to the margin that is closest, and write the English word at the end of that line. Continue this

process until you have translated every word that you are unfamiliar with. In the end, because it is a topic that interests you, it will make it that much easier to converse on this same subject later.

Step #7 to Reading for Results: Internalize the Lesson
For one week, use this same article. While internalizing the meaning, read it aloud five times each day, whether consecutive or spaced out. This will help to solidify the information and make you think in Spanish about the topic. You will develop proper rhythm and tempo in your speaking abilities as well, but that's not all.

As you continue to follow this method, you will begin to find that other aspects of your Spanish abilities begin to improve automatically. You will find it easier and easier to effortlessly express your ideas regarding the topic, and you will discover you are better able to pronounce those words that gave you trouble.

Doing this for the first week should open your eyes to the effectiveness of using articles to develop your Spanish fluency. But this is just the beginning. Now it time to delve even deeper.

Step #8 to Reading for Results: Bringing It Together

You should have already made a list of things you would like to talk about, in Spanish, with native speakers. In fact, if you're putting into practice what you're learning in Mission Trip Spanish, you've probably had a few discussions on those things already. Let's go deeper and further your knowledge and abilities by using that list here.

Look up articles that are related to the topics you would like to talk about. Use the same news website that you used for the first article. Again, you should find that it piques your interest to know what the story is all about. For me, I often like to learn about topics that have to do with criminal justice, history, and major events that occur in the country. Of course, not only am I interested in these kinds of topics, but the people who live in the country that I am visiting are also very interested in these topics because they are living them!

So find your next article and follow the exact same method you did the first time. You should be able to do one article per week for every week before your mission trip to Latin America. If so, when it comes time for you to step on that plane, you will have revised at least five full articles with authentic Spanish that you have added to your arsenal. When you arrive, you can surprise the people that you meet with your knowledge of current events in their country and your ability to speak freely about your opinions regarding the topics. Not only can you have this ability, but you should be able to speak better, in general, because of your constant practice and time spent with the language.

But wait, there's more. This is only one powerful aspect of the method meant to prepare you for your mission trip to Latin America. While you are reading your articles in Spanish, you will be doing other things to prepare. In the next chapter, I will show you how to use songs in order to take your Spanish and your cultural understanding of it to the next level. I'm not talking about Pitbull or Shakira (although they both have some catchy tunes). I am talking about increasing your understanding of the Spanish spoken in the country that you are visiting. This powerful tool will continue to maximize the fun that you have in learning Spanish, and make your experience in the country absolutely amazing.

Chapter 5: Using Songs the Right Way

You are probably familiar with the common practice among Spanish teachers and in language-learning top- ten list articles that suggest you listen to songs by Ricky Martin, Shakira, and other artists who sing in both English and Spanish. Perhaps you've heard this advice and promptly started listening to songs without a clue about how to start using them to improve your Spanish. The "experts" told you all you have to do is listen to them in the car, listen to them in the elevator and listen to them in the grocery store check-out line. I don't know about you, but I am mighty distracted when I am on my 30 second elevator ride, on the rare occasion that I use an elevator. I'm busy driving when I'm in the car, and I am willing to bet that four minutes of distracted grocery cart emptying one day a week is not the golden time to soak up new language information.

Cliché advice will just serve to frustrate you. Mission Trip Spanish has the proper method to learning Spanish quickly through music. When you combine this method over the next five weeks along with your speaking and reading assignments, you will see dramatic results in your comprehension and overall fluency. That is, you will be WAY better at speaking Spanish with the locals and those who you are serving than if you had skipped this step.

First, think about the songs in your life that have been the most memorable songs. These will not necessarily be your favorite songs, but they will be the most catchy songs. They were usually pretty upbeat, and the lyrics were captivating and easy enough to you for you to remember without much effort. This is the basis for the technique that I will show you when it comes to using songs to learn Spanish quickly.

Now think of the country that you live in. Think of the region of that country. Surely there are some songs that you identify with. There are songs that you have heard over and over since you were a child, and there are songs that you currently listen to on a regular basis, or at the very least, you hear other people listening to them. This same thing happens in the country you will be visiting. There are certain songs that everyone knows, songs that everyone is currently listening to. Thus if you find out which songs are popular in the country you will be visiting, you will be able to do three things at once! You will be able to learn songs that you will likely hear when you arrive in the country, you will learn authentic Spanish as it is known and spoken in that country, and you will be listening to a new song that you might actually enjoy.

How It Works: Using Music to Improve Language Skills

How do you go about finding the song, learning the words, and finally understanding what is being said? All it takes is a few simple tools that you probably already have access to.

Step #1 to Using Music for Learning: Find Artists
First, visit your favorite search engine in order to find bands, artists or songs from the country in which you will be serving.

Step #2 to Using Music for Learning: Ask About the Most Popular Songs
Once you have identified a number of possible song choices, start asking around about which songs are the best. Remember the chapter about speaking to people and the one about using websites and apps? Songs are one of many ways that those lessons will pay off. Ask the kind person you met on Italki.com about the most popular or well-known songs from his

or her country. People love to talk about where they are from, but they love to talk about music even more! So it should be pretty easy to come up with a list of songs that are winners for your Spanish learning. You may be thinking that you need a whole grocery list, but at first, only choose two or three songs that you have listened to and really like. These will become the basis for your learning over the next couple of weeks, when it comes to Spanish songs.

Step #3 to Using Music for Learning: Search for the Lyrics
Now that you have your songs, it is time to figure out what they mean. Go to your search engine, type in the song title and also type in "letras" after it. Then search. You will then find websites that have clearly laid out the song for you to read while you listen. Now copy and paste these Spanish lyrics into a blank document for your Dropbox. Next, search for the English translation of the song. You should find a translation that has already been done. DO NOT USE A TRANSLATOR WEBSITE. That completely defeats the purpose, as you want to know that the meaning is accurate. Instead, go to your new friend from Italki.com and ask if they can help you understand each line.

Step #4 to Using Music for Learning: Retaining Rhythm and Words
As you go through the process of understanding the song, you will subconsciously begin to retain the words and rhythm without trying. This is what you want to happen! Just like when you read articles, your brain will retain information from the songs when you listen to them as often as you can, especially because you've used the simple, catchy ones.

Follow Steps #1-4 over the next five weeks (and even after you get back from your mission trip).

Chapter 6: Movies: Fun, Free, and Motivating
Using movies to improve your Spanish is one of the best ways to be speaking and understanding in time for your mission trip. Noticed something? Mission Trip Spanish combines the most powerful methods into an intense, and fun, immersion package. Thus far, you have found someone in your destination country to talk to regularly; you are studying interesting articles from that country; you are also listening to and

learning from the top music being sung there. You will find your brain is being adjusted to accept a new culture and tongue.

Watching a movie in Spanish is the closest, most immediate way to open yourself up to the place you will visit, without even having to leave your room. Think how powerful this can be for your Spanish learning! Think of the motivation you will get from watching movies in Spanish, understanding things better and better every time you watch a new movie, and gaining a whole new list of new words and phrases that are actually used in everyday life! There are SO many words and phrases that you will never find in a textbook, workbook, or phrasebook that you will nonetheless find in everyday speech. This makes it truly amazing how much your Spanish can improve in a short period of time, if you follow the Mission Spanish Trip method.

And you can watch whatever movies you feel like watching at the time. If you want drama, you can have it. Comedy? You can find that too! Even if you feel that you are too tired, too busy or too lazy on any given day, just pick a movie you think looks pretty good in Spanish and let your brain do the rest! Now do not go thinking that I want you to do any passive watching. There is a method to everything, and this one will stimulate your brain and make the words, phrases, accent, and culture come together for you in a way that studying a book cannot.

Think about what happens when you are watching a movie. You hear the actor's voice, you see the actor talking, and you get to view a scene that mirrors what might occur in real life. Honestly, some of my best moments in Spanish learning have come while I watched a movie. I can still remember some nights while I was in graduate school, fatigued from working on research papers and studying all day. I would pick a random movie I had found on the internet and would instantly be entertained, all while increasing my knowledge of Spanish.

I invite you conduct a test to see whether the Mission Trip Spanish method is working better than language software, crossword puzzles, or workbooks. Simply ask someone who exclusively relies on those methods to come watch a movie with you. See if they can understand as much as you do about what is going on in the movie. Once you realize just how powerful this tool is to your Spanish learning, you will be even more motivated to use it and the other techniques in this book in order to increase your Spanish learning rapidly.

For the vigilant language learner, a movie can be one of the best tools to help you with every part of your Spanish learning.

So choose something you will enjoy. Once you start hearing the characters speak, you will begin to think about what they are saying and you will even hear words that you've never heard before. When you hear some of these words or phrases, write them down! All you have to do is pause the movie for a moment and write down the word or the phrase that you did not understand. Later, go ask your language partner what it means. Then if you feel that that word or phrase is worth keeping, add it to your master list for your mission trip!

Now you must be thinking, "I don't know where to find a Spanish movie, and I don't have the money to purchase one, if I did."

Never fear! That is what this book is here to address. I am going to tell you the exact steps you need to take in order to find free movies from your destination country!

How It Works: Finding Spanish Movies for Free

There are a number of excellent websites on the Internet that you can access right now and begin watching movies in Spanish for free. Unfortunately, it can be very hard to find where these gems are hidden unless you have been doing this for a while. Luckily, I have been finding them for you over the years, mainly because I use them myself!

Let's get going with the method.

Step #1 to Getting the Best Out of Movies: As Always, Focus on the Destination Country
It should be no surprise to you that the Spanish you hear from one country is different from that of another. Often, countries that are geographically located in very close proximity can still vary widely on the words and phrases that are used. For example: Argentina and Bolivia are often noted as having vastly different styles of speech and common phrases.

Once you have decided what kind of movies you like, ask your language partner from that country if she or he has any suggestions on the most popular titles from that country. Your language partner is one of the most valuable ways to tap into a wealth of knowledge. He or she will be able to tell you what the locals like, what is considered a good movie for their standards, and might even recommend some movies that you never even thought of. This has happened to me on numerous occasions, and every time I am blown away at how good movies from foreign countries are! For example: one of my favorite actors is the Argentine comedian Guillermo Francella. Think of the Spanish-speaking equivalent of Steve Martin. I LOVE this guy's movies, and I honestly consider some of his films to be as dear to me as A Christmas Story is to my grandfather or Halloween Town is to my little brother.

If you let the power of movie watching work for you, I promise you will be just as glad as I am that you added this to your Spanish learning strategy. So take the movie suggestions from your language partner, or embrace your favorite genre at the moment and start using a search engine. Look up which movies look good and make a note of the ones that you found.

Step #2 to Getting the Best Out of Movies: Head to YouTube.com.

You can see if the movies on your list are free by going to YouTube. Often, older movies or movies that are no longer being produced make their way onto Youtube. You can take advantage of this for your language-learning! Similar to what you did with your newspaper search, go to YouTube.com and type into your search bar the following: "Movies from (country you will visit)." You will find that there are a number of full length movies that will come up. Perhaps these look good, perhaps not. Now search for the usernames of those who uploaded the films that you thought looked good. Usually that same person has uploaded more than just one movie. Go see if there are any other movies that they have uploaded that look good. Write those down in your list. Rinse and repeat.

Step #3 to Getting the Best Out of Movies: Try ForeignFilms
Go to ForeignFilms.com. You will be able to search the titles by country. See which ones you like that are from the country where you will visit, and see if they are available for free.

Step #4 to Getting the Best Out of Movies: Cruise Over to Netflix

If you have an account with Netflix.com, do a search there for the suggested titles that you got from your language partner. You can also simply enter the name of the country you will be visiting into the search engine. This may help you to uncover some hidden gems that you may not have known were out there. Also, just as an aside, most movies on Netflix can be watched in Spanish. Simply do a search for how to change the language of a movie using your device and you're done!

Finally, review your list. By now, you will easily have between fifteen and twenty solid titles that you will likely enjoy and find educational at the same time. Just like that, you have created your very own personalized library of Spanish movies to watch, and all from the destination country you will be visiting! Instead of struggling to hunt down movies to buy, you now have everything you need.

How It Works: Learning New Words and Phrases while Watching Movies

So you've picked your movie and your screen is ready to go. Before you press play, just make sure you've got just a few items ready to help you to capture words and phrases with ease while enjoying the plot and action of the movie.

1. Grab your phone and make sure you have the apps for WordReference, Reverso, and a note taking app ready. If you do not have a smartphone, open WordReference and Reverso on your computer along with note-taking software.
2. Start watching the movie! Get into the storyline, but stop whenever you hear something that catches your ear that you have heard before and wanted to know what it meant. Also pause to write down whatever you think might be useful.
3. While the movie is on pause, search that term or phrase in WordReference or Reverso. You will likely be able to find the word or phrase rapidly. Now make a note of the meaning, then keep watching.
4. Keep this up for the whole movie, stopping wherever you feel you need or want to.
5. By the end of the movie you should have ten or twenty really good words or phrases that will help you a lot on your way. Simply

add these to your master list of words that you would like to learn, and you're done.

As a side note, on my phone, I have allowed the voice-to-text feature to be in English and Spanish. This means that if I do not have a clue how to spell a word, I simply repeat the word as well as I can, and the software understands what I am trying to say 99% of the time. It's brilliant!

Whichever exercise you are doing from Mission Trip Spanish, make sure to add all the words and phrases into your master list, whether on your phone, computer, or in your Dropbox. Whenever you need new words to memorize, simply draw from your master list and you are ready to move forward with your personalized studies.

Later in the book, I will tell you how language experts memorize words and phrases. If you follow the Mission Trip Spanish method for memorization, you can see a dramatic transformation in your spoken Spanish.

But before that, it is equally important to preach to the choir about what is often considered the "most important part" of language-learning. I've got a few things for you to know about the "most important part," and I hope that you will keep it in mind the next time that someone asks you. I am talking, of course, about daily practice.

Chapter 7: Daily Practice: "The Most Important Part"

Excuse the rant, but daily practice has been echoed everywhere as the key to success in every arena. Some have even gone so far as to say that it is the "most important part" when it comes to learning anything new. This simply isn't true.

I know a cliché when I see one. And I don't want you to be another victim of the mythical tale of the person who did the same thing every single day for years and then suddenly became successful at it. The definition of insanity remains, "Doing the same thing over and over again and expecting different results."

As you can tell, I am not the greatest fan of the myth that the ONLY thing it takes to succeed at your goal of learning Spanish is to practice some incredibly boring task every single day. When I hear this rhetoric, my mind inevitably races to a mental image of someone grinding it out, no matter how much they hate the method they've chosen, whether it's completing yet another crossword puzzle or verb conjugation chart. Now, does this mean that I encourage you to blow off your language-learning all together? NO! ABSOLUTELY- N.O.!

What I am saying is that the mindset should never be that you must do the same routine over and over and over again until you snap out of your haze and realize that you have miraculous powers.

Instead, I want you to start thinking of your Spanish learning in this way: Focus on doing what inspires you, what motivates you, what interests you. Do you see the difference? One is a slow, monotonous, dull, soul-sucking outlook on learning Spanish, while the other speaks to your humanness. We are people after all! We want to do what we find fascinating, stimulating and motivating. So instead of thinking that your success in learning Spanish for your mission trip is dependent on some unwavering robot-like willpower, relax. If you're on your way out of the country in a little over a month, of course you will need to put in some time every day, but that doesn't mean banging your head against the wall.

Remember this: don't tie yourself down to studying the same exact way every single day. You have to keep it interesting. Mix up your learning according to what you are inclined to work on each day. If you simply make sure that you keep your Spanish materials within arm's reach during all of your entertainment time, fun time, diligent time, and relaxation time, you will have the right kind of Spanish learning resource you need at any time.

So the next time someone tells you that you are doomed to hunker down behind a pile of workbooks and Spanish learning software, you can rest easy knowing that your method is a whole lot more fun and effective than that. In fact, you'll be amazed at how other people will tend to be discouraged and give up, while you breeze along, loving the heck out of your new language and loving every minute of your journey towards full fluency, if that is your goal.

Once you've seen the beauty of communicating with those you serve on a mission trip, you will probably come back home more determined to improve beyond proficiency and into fluency. Most people experience how rewarding the results of Mission Trip Spanish are, and are ready to continue applying it in order to continue into higher levels of fluency.

Now that you've heard all about the merits of Mission Trip Spanish, you're probably wondering how you are supposed to memorize the new words and phrases that you'll find in this book and those you've gathered from songs, movies, your language partner and beyond. In the next chapter, I will lay out how you can memorize words and phrases very fast. I present these to you after a ton of trial and error, and many were tailored from memorization theories. In the end, this is the memorization method that continues to work for me and for those who I have helped in their Spanish learning journey. All of these work well, but if you find that one of these memorization technique works particularly well for you, use it exclusively.

Chapter 8: No-Fluff Memorization Techniques

When it comes to memorizing for your mission trip to a Spanish-speaking country, both the short term memory and the long term memory will come into play. When you are communicating with someone, you often need to be able to use your short term memory to remember things that you are talking about, while at the same time using your long term memory to recall words or phrases that you learned five weeks ago.

Using rote memorization on its own will allow you to retain a lot of information, but only for a short amount of time, perhaps just long enough to pass a test. Here, we are not trying to pass a test, rather we are trying to develop a lasting ability to connect us with our fellow human beings.

There are a variety of methods that language-learning experts use in order retain information in a short amount of time, while being able to keep the words and phrases in their long-term memory. In this chapter, I will show you the exact techniques that these language experts use. If you use these techniques wisely, you will find that you too have the ability to learn a large number of words and phrases, and you will be able to remember what you learned while you are on your mission trip.

Simply put, the Mission Trip Spanish method of memorization is designed for you to get results in a short amount of time so that you can start speaking Spanish right away.

Memorization Tip # 1: The Memory List
To get started, use your master list and make a separate list of all of the words and phrases that you have committed to memory using deliberate learning. If you have completely memorized any of the material in your master list, add it. This is your "done" list.

From the remaining words, make a separate list of those words that still need to be memorized. This is your memory list. While you are constructing your memory list, make sure that the words and phrases are those that you can actually see yourself needing while you are on your mission trip. If you try to add words that have no use to you at the moment, you may find that your interest and attention levels are not very high. When it comes to choosing what you want to memorize, interest is key. If you do not have any interest in the material that you are learning, your brain will reject the information as irrelevant.

Your memory list should be designed in a way that you can easily view and review ten pieces of information per day using this method --an ideal number. If you consider the amount of time that you have left until your mission trip, perhaps five weeks, you will potentially be able to commit to memory up to 350 words and phrases in that time using only this list! One of the best parts about using the list is that you decide what goes into it. So when you think of that 350 word and phrase count, think of a memory list filled with well thought-out and precise words and phrases that are specifically designed for you to communicate with those you serve while on your mission trip. That is some powerful stuff that you just will not find in software or in verb conjugation charts.

How It Works: Making Your Memory List

Make your memory list using a word processor. I find that this method works best for me, as I can link it to my Dropbox account and keep it with me wherever I go. Also keep a hard copy of the list for easy reference and review. If you didn't start a master list in the beginning, just add them to your memory list as you go along --ten new words or phrases at a time, which you are gathering from your language partner, a movie, or other sources. Here are the details on how to format your memory list:

1. Always make sure to add a sentence that gives the word or phrase some context. Context is extremely important when it comes to learning new vocabulary and phrases because it will allow you to recall the information when you need it most.
2. Make sure your paper has two columns, one for English (far right side) and the other side for Spanish (far left side).
3. Date the top of the page so you know when you learned the words. This will also help later when you are working on the spaced repetition technique.
4. Make sure that there are exactly ten words or phrases per page. This helps you to keep up with your progress and to encourage you to aim for more and more words committed to memory for life. All you have to do is continue adding to your list.

In this book, I have included a list of words and phrases that will serve you well while you are on your mission trip to Latin America. You may use these words and phrases to get you started, or you can substitute them with your own words and phrases that you believe will help you the most. If you decide that you want to continue your Spanish journey after you return from your trip, simply come back to this chapter and review this material. It will give you a starting point for your life-long Spanish journey. Whether you want to learn Spanish for your mission trip or for life, the tools are the same. Here, I will give you some of the most effective memorization techniques that are used by language experts to permanently learn many words and phrases in a short amount of time.

Keep this list on hand. You will be using it with the techniques below.

Memorization Tip #2: Mnemonics
When learning memory recall, one of the tried and true methods is to use mnemonic devices. It is possibly the single most powerful strategy used to memorize. Around this one technique, you can add extra steps to make your recall incredibly effective. In this section, I will outline how to make your list truly your own and how you can learn the words and phrases there for life.

A mnemonic device is a method or technique that helps you to remember information rapidly and for a long period of time. This is a method that you can use to increase your fluency extremely fast. It is used by memory champs and graduate students in order to learn words, phrases, and other information very fast and for a very long time.

How It Works: Using Mnemonics for Language-Learning

1. Decide on your list of ten words or phrases that you would like to memorize for today.
2. Once you have your phrases, go to a quiet place so that you can practice aloud
3. Fold your paper in half so that one side has Spanish and the other side has English
4. Say your first word or phrase out loud (in Spanish) and look at the definition, go down the list in a similar way
5. When you have completed this exercise, repeat until you have done this five times.
6. Now start with the other side (the English side) and try to recall the Spanish equivalent aloud
7. Continue this until you have done it five times

Be sure to really concentrate and give it your best. You will find it fun when you give it your all!

Now that you have gotten your brain into the swing of things, it is time to go back to the first word or phrase using the visualization technique outlined in the next section.

Memorization Tip #3: Visualization

Look at the first term on the Spanish side and try to think of the sounds in chunks. For example:

The Spanish translation of national holiday is feriado nacional. Think "Fair-ree-auto Naw-see-own-owl." Now use your brain to come up with an English word that you associate with each of those sounds. It could be that you think of: a county fair, a car that reeks, a seeing-eye dog, and a night owl. Perhaps your brain has done something else with these sounds. This is a highly personalized exercise.

Now try to create an image in your head using these words so that you can recreate the term in your mind. For example, you might think of a county fair you attended when you were little. Think about how you felt, the smell of the cow pies, the heat of the summer night. Think back and remember that you are at this fair during a national holiday, perhaps the 4th of July. Now think about a car driving through the middle of the fair, it is filled with those cow pies you smelled. The smell is getting stronger as it gets closer. As the car approaches you, you can see that the car is being pulled by a seeing-eye dog and that the driver is actually an owl! The owl is the size of a man and is wearing a Hawaiian shirt because he is on vacation, it is a national holiday after all. Now, think about the sounds again, "Fair-ree-auto Naw-see-own-all." Close your eyes and think about it for ten full seconds, replaying the scene in your mind and connecting each sound to its English word in your story. Open your eyes.

What just happened? You just burned into your memory the meaning of feriado nacional. By now you have conjured up in your mind a scene so bizarre, so outlandish, that it is actually hard to get the idea of smelling cow pies out of your mind. This is because you have just exercised what experts commonly refer to as the mind's eye. This concept refers to your spatial (visual) memory which is considered to be much more effective than your verbal memory.

The idea behind it is that when we create an outlandish story using the sounds of the words, we are able to recall the story, which reminds us of the different sounds of the words. As you get better and better at this technique, you will find that it takes you less and less time to come up with a story to go along with your words. Also, keep in mind that once you have committed the word to your long term memory, you will simply remember the word without the story attached. When this happens, you have truly committed this word or phrase to your memory, it is yours.

Now sometimes even this method is not enough for you to fully memorize words or phrases you are having trouble with. This can happen when you are trying to learn many words that center around one topic, or when you want to learn a lot of information in a particular order. This is when the next memorization technique comes in.

Memorization Tip #4: The Roman Room

This technique is a method that you can use to remember words and phrases in order. This method also takes advantage of your mind's eye and uses your spatial memory to recall chunks of information. I will give you an example of how this method may be used, and then I encourage you to personalize this technique for yourself. Don't be alarmed if it seems similar to the visualization you were just given, above. The Roman room seems similar, and is, because it expands on the visualization technique and makes it more powerful. It may also be applied to other forms of memorization, such as lists of information, like the itinerary for your mission trip week. It involves committing information to memory by "pegging" the words or phrases to objects in your mind. The exact place in your brain is called the Roman room or memory palace.

This method is said to have its origins in ancient Rome during a time when knowledge was passed down orally. At the time, it was necessary to remember a lot of information because books were not readily available. Today, it is used by language experts to learn and retain large amounts of information.

How It Works: Using Your Imagination

1. Imagine a place that you know very well. For most people it is their home, school, workplace, or morning commute.
2. Think about the route that you take while you go through your well known place. Think of the different rooms, the different areas where you might stop, and other memorable locations.
3. Now that you have a place in mind, make sure that whenever you think of your place, you start in the same place, and you go through the same route in your mind every single time.
4. Now it's time to add your information. Think of a few words that you are trying to learn. For example, you may want to be able to recall the meaning of the Spanish phrases: feriado nacional (remember?) and jaqueca (migraine). Now imagine that you are walking into the front door of your house. You open the door and standing in front of you is a clown from the fair. He has been sent by the government to remind you that today is a national holiday. He hands you a unicycle and ushers you into your living room. Once inside, the clown begins to stand on your coffee table with

his giant red shoes. You are horrified because the clown might break your table! You then ask the clown to get down. In response, the clown starts to sing the national anthem loudly, and tries to get you to join in, too. At this point, you are thoroughly confused. That is, until you realize that today is a national holiday and that the clown is just here to remind you that you should go to the fair because you do not have to work or go to school!

5. After the clown is done, you go into your kitchen in to get some water, you have developed a bad migraine after hearing the clown sing the national anthem so loudly. When you walk into the kitchen, you see that something looks funny about your refrigerator. It actually looks like the handle to the fridge is HOT! It's so hot that it's burning red. You need some water though, so you open it anyway. It burns you because it is actually hot when you open the fridge door. Just as you open the door, tons of CAKE come pouring out of the refrigerator. It's getting all over you, the floor and the kitchen appliances! Quickly, you think about how you are going to fix this mess and remember that you have a lot of extra space in your CAR to put all of the CAKE that has come out of the HOT refrigerator. You go to your car, open the trunk, and start filling. As you fill the car with cake, you realize that your migraine headache is still not going away. You then leave your car and run down the driveway get some water somewhere else, leaving the HOT refrigerator that's in the house, the CAKE that is all over the place, and your CAR in the driveway as you run to the store for some migraine medicine. HOT-CAKE-CAR = Ja-que-ca (Migraine)

Have you noticed a pattern when it comes to using these techniques? The pattern is that they all build on themselves. When you use visualization with emotion, places, feelings, smell, sound, touch, taste, etc., it all becomes very hard to get out of your memory. You are breaking the word down into its most basic sounds so that you can attach English words to them for quicker and more lasting recall. That is exactly what we want to happen. Also, keep in mind that, just as with plain visualization, you will get faster at coming up with stories and images with practice. For example, I have been using this technique for so long that I am able to come up with outlandish stories that stick in my memory in just a few moments. You will be able to do the same with a little practice.

There is one extra method that you should keep in mind when memorizing for your mission trip. That is the power of spaced repetition. This method, coupled with the techniques we just covered, will make the words and phrases that you learn stick in your head with ease. This makes it vital to preparing for your upcoming mission trip.

Memorization Tip #5: Spaced Repetition

Spaced repetition is central to retaining all of the information that you are learning in a short period of time.

Remember, as with any successful memorization technique, there should be a "done" list that contains all of the words and phrases that you have already learned, and a memory list that has the words you are going to learn.

Of course, I will teach you exactly what you need to know about using your memory list to memorize using spaced repetition.

How It Works: Using Spaced Repetition

Look back to the section regarding your list. Remember how I said to put the date at the top of each page of 10 words or phrases? This is the point where those dates come in handy.

This is how you should proceed with your list using those dates:

1. On the first day, memorize your first ten words and phrases using the memorization techniques mentioned above.
2. On the second day, memorize the second set of words and phrases. Now go back and review the words from day one.
3. On the third day, memorize the third set of words and phrases. Now go back and review the words from day two and day one.
4. Repeat this until you reach day seven. On that day, review for all seven days.
5. Once you reach day seven, put those seven sets aside and start learning the next week's words and phrases in the same way as the first week.

6. When you reach the end of the second week, review your whole week and then review the first week's materials again. You will find that your ability to recall is very strong! This is the spaced repetition method working its magic. Keep this up until the day you leave for your mission trip. Once you reach that day, you will be more than prepared for what lies ahead.

This method of memorization is so straightforward and works incredibly well for everyone to whom I have taught it. Give it a try, and become part of the success story.

Memorization Tip #6: The Pomodoro Technique

This technique has many varieties, but very often is known as the 25-5 technique. I use a modified version of this, the 10-5. "Pomodoro" is the Italian word for tomato. Let me explain. There once was a university student in the 1980s who was trying to figure out the optimal amount of time to study in a very concentrated manner. This student, Francesco Cirillo, determined that he could concentrate very well for about 25 minutes at a time. He also found that he could take a break in between studying for about 5 minutes. The "pomodoro" part of the name comes from the tomato shaped kitchen timer that he used to keep himself on track. An added bonus that Cirillo found is that when the timer ticked, it seemed to create a sense of urgency, which allowed him to stay concentrated on his task. For our purposes the task would be memorization using visualization, the Roman room or spaced repetition.

I have personally used this method while learning, because I have found that if I am not giving all my concentration, I may not learn as quickly as I would like. Many people[7] are the same way. Keep in mind, you have ten words to learn today, and then tomorrow, and then the next day! Therefore, you had better pay attention when you learn them the first time. Luckily, when you add this technique to all of the other memorization techniques we have covered, you will find that memorizing new terms comes very naturally, and without much difficulty, thanks to the system you now have set up.

And those are the memorization techniques! You now know about the most effective methods of memorization. Now that you have reviewed them, you are probably wondering how much time you need to devote to memorizing in the first place. As a general rule, make sure to only memorize ten words or phrases a day because retention is optimal at this number. If you choose a different number, still make sure that you are consistent and that you are memorizing every single day. Remember, you only have five weeks, so make these five weeks count. I guarantee that you will see the rewards of your dedication once you arrive in the country where you will be serving.

Again, what is normally considered "daily practice" --hunching for hours over mind-stiffening verb conjugation charts, is counterproductive. The Mission Trip Spanish method is to:

1. Focus on memorization for no more than an hour each day
2. Speak with your language partner for as long as you would like (most people love to keep talking and talking when they are excited about learning)
3. Read your articles for about thirty minutes per day.
4. You can also watch movies or listen to songs.

Got it? So now you have a flexible, varied schedule of interesting ways to learn Spanish in five weeks.

"But Tyler! That will take up a lot of my time!" Well, you may be right if you were planning on doing all of this in one huge chunk at the end of the day, but in reality you can break this up throughout your day. It has two great effects when I do so. It keeps my Spanish mind fresh all day, and it makes it seem less like I am studying and more like I am living my Spanish-speaking lifestyle. So give it a try, and break up all of these parts throughout your day. You will be very glad you did. Remember, after these five weeks, you should have learned all of the words and phrases you will need, and your ear should be very tuned and able to understand native speakers. Be ready to connect with your fellow human beings while on your mission trip. Think of your goals and keep your eye on the prize! In the next chapter, I will actually give you words and phrases that you can add to your list right now in order to get started right away.

Chapter 9: Mission Trip Phrases (Use These and Add Your Own)
The words and phrases below are all authentic and come from Nicaragua. If you are going to serve in another part of Latin America and would like to

use these words and phrases, just be sure to ask your language partner how they would be said in his/her country. You can add some (or all) of these words and phrases to your list. If you are simply using this book for the list and you flipped straight to this chapter, I will add a word of caution. Remember that just because you can read the Spanish part and figure out what it is saying, it does not mean that you will be able to recall that information from memory, immediately, while you are trying to connect with someone on your mission trip. Make sure to use the memorization techniques from earlier in the book in order to burn these words and phrases into your memory. You will be very glad that you did. So without further ado, here is a starter list for learning Spanish for your mission trip.

The Mission Trip Spanish Starter List:

Greetings and Meetings
Hello, it's nice to meet you. *Hola, mucho gusto.*

I'm sorry, I didn't catch your name. *Disculpe, no agarre tu nombre.*

Do you know each other? *Se conocen el uno con el otro?/Se* conocen?

We go to church together. *Vamos a la Iglesia juntos./Vamos juntos a la iglesia.*

How long have you lived here? *Desde cuándo vives aquí?/Cuánto tiempo has vivido aquí?*

How long do you plan on staying here? *Cuánto tiempo planeas quedarte?/Cuánto tiempo estarás aquí?*

Do you like it here? *Te gusta aqui?*

What do you like about it? *Qué es lo que te gusta?/Que te gusta?*

Who do you live with? *Con quién vives?*

Do you go to church here? *Vas a la iglesia aquí?*

We just got here. *Ya llegamos.*

How are you? *Cómo estás?/Qué tal?*

Hello, my name is... *Hola! Me llamo.../Mi nombre es...*

Describing Yourself and Others

I came here to work and help out. *Vine a trabajar y ayudar./Vine a echarles una mano.*

We all go to the same church. *Vamos a la misma iglesia./Nos congregamos en la misma iglesia.*

I live outside the big city. It's near the city of Atlanta, in the state of Georgia. *Vivo lejos de la gran ciudad. Es cerca de Atlanta, en el estado de Georgia.*

I am in high school. *Estoy en secundaria.*

I am just here to help. *Estoy aquí para ayudar.*

She is very nice. *Ella es amable/agradable.*

He is a little grumpy today. *El es un poco malhumorado.*

She is in a good mood. *Ella está de buenas.*

He is in a bad mood. *Él está de malas.*

I just want to help people. *Solo quiero ayudar a la gente.*

I am _____ years old. *Tengo ____ años de edad.*

I like soccer and basketball. *Me gusta el fútbol y el basketball.*

The Family

I come from a large family. *Vengo de una familia grande.*

I am an only child. *Soy hijo unico.*

I spend a lot of time with my family, just like you guys. *Gasto mucho tiempo con mi familia, como ustedes chicos.*

My grandparents are from Italy/ Spain/ Puerto Rico/ Europe. *Mis abuelos son de Italia/España/Puerto Rico/Europa.*

I am Native American. *Soy nativo de América.*

I am scots-Irish. *Soy escoceses-irlandeses.*

I have one older sister and one younger brother. *Tengo una hermana mayor y un hermano menor.*

I am one of two twins. *Soy uno de los gemelos.*

My family usually eats dinner together. *Mi familia usualmente comen juntos.*

We eat a lot of meat in my family. *Comemos mucha carne en mi familia.*

I have a lot of family members all over the country. *Tengo mucha familia en todo el país.*

Do you have any other pets? *Tienes alguna otra mascota?*

Weather

It is really sunny out today. *Está soleado hoy.*

What is the temperature right now? *Cuál es la temperatura ahora?*

What's the forecast? *Cuál es el pronóstico?*

It looks like it is going to rain soon. *Parece que lloverá pronto.*

It's supposed to clear up later. *Se supone que aclarar después.*

What a beautiful day! *Que lindo dia!*

It is humid today. *Está húmedo hoy.*

It is very hot today. *Está caliente hoy.*

It is windy. *Está ventoso hoy.*

It's bad weather. *Hace mal tiempo.*

The sky is overcast. *El cielo está nublado.*

The sun is coming out. *El sol está saliendo.*

The volcano spews ash and lava when it erupts. *El volcán arroja ceniza y lava cuando entra en erupción.*

Earthquake. *Terremoto.*

A big storm is moving in. *Viene una gran tormenta.*

Are there tornados here? *Hay tornados aqui?*

Has there been a drought? *Hay una sequia?*

Is it going to flood? *Va a inundar?*

Playing Sports

I'm the best soccer/tennis/basketball player you have ever seen. *Soy el mejor futbolista/jugador de tenis/jugador de basketball que has visto.*

I'm not really a big fan of sports, but I'll give it a try! *No soy fanático del deporte pero lo intentaré.*

What is the score? *Como quedo?/Cual es la puntuación?*

Who won? *Quién ganó?*

It was a tie! *Empatados!*

What time is the game on (the radio or television)? *A qué hora es el juego?*

Pass it to me! *Pasamelo!*

I'm open! *Soy todos oídos. Estoy abierto!*

I get a free kick (penalty kick). *Tengo un penal.*

I got fouled! *Me hicieron una falta!*

It's just a game. *Solo es un juego.*

My favorite team is... *Mi equipo favorito es...*

What is your favorite team? *Cuál es tu equipo favorito?*

Do you like Barcelona, Real Madrid, Chelsea? *Te gusta el Barcelona, Real Madrid, Chelsea?*

Construction Projects

I am ready to get to work! *Estoy listo para trabajar!*

What are we doing here? *Qué hacemos aquí?*

We are digging trenches. *Estamos cavando trincheras.*

When do we lay down the pipes? *Cuándo nos acostamos las tuberías?*

Do I cover it with dirt? *Lo cubro con tierra?*

What happens if it rains? *Qué pasa si llueve?*

I'm willing to help wherever I am needed. *Estoy dispuesto a ayudar siempre que me necesiten.*

Just tell me where to go. *Solo dime a donde ir.*

Do I need to bring any tools? *Necesito traer herramientas?*

Break time. *Tiempo de descanso/receso.*

Where can I find a hammer and nails? *Dónde puedo encontrar un martillo y clavos?*

We are building a house. *Estamos haciendo una casa.*

We are cleaning up the house. *Estamos limpiando la casa.*

We are pouring concrete for the foundation. *Estamos vertiendo concreto para los cimientos.*

Do you need any help over here? *Necesitas ayuda por aquí?*

We are going to install flushing toilets. *Instalaremos inodoros.*

I need to drink more water. *Necesito beber más agua.*

Does anyone have a shovel? *Alguién tiene una pala?*

I hope the project is finished soon! *Espero que el proyecto termine pronto.*

Where is the water source? *Dónde está la fuente de agua?*

Medical/Hospital

I have a broken foot. *Tengo el pie quebrado.*

Do you have a heating pad? *Tienes una almohada de calefacción?*

I have high blood pressure. *Tengo la presion alta.*

Do you have a fever? *Tienes calentura/fiebre?*

How long have you been feeling sick? *Desde cuándo te sientes enfermo?*

I have a migraine headache. *Tengo migraña/jaqueca.*

Altitude sickness. *Enfermedad de altitud.*

Could you please call a doctor? *Puedes llamar a un doctor por favor?*

I have diarrhea. *Tengo diarrea.*

I am constipated. *Tengo constipado.*

Can the doctor or nurse come here? *Puede un doctor o enfermera venir?*

Not Feeling Too Well

Is there a bathroom where we are going? *Hay un baño donde vamos?*

Is there a bathroom on the way? *Hay un baño en el camino?*

Do you have any tums/antacids? *Tienes algún tums/antiácido?*

I don't feel well. *No me siento bien.*

Do you have any headache medicine? *Tienes medicina para el dolor de cabeza?*

I have a really bad headache. *Tengo un mal dolor de cabeza.*

Do you have a tissue? *Tiene un panuelo/panueleta?*

I feel dizzy. *Me siento mareado.*

I feel sore today. *Me siento adolorido hoy.*

My stomach hurts. *Me duele el estomago/la panza.*

Fun Activities

What do we have planned for today? *Qué plan tenemos para hoy?*

I can't wait to get there! *No puedo aguantar para llegar!*

Are you guys playing jump rope? *Chicos, están jugando a la cuerda?*

What kind of game is this? *Que tipo de juego es este?*

Do you want to play a game of soccer? *Quieres jugar un partido de fútbol?*

Do you want to play a card game? *Quieres jugar naipe?*

Do you want to play board games? *Quieres jugar tablero?*

We are going to go on a hike. *Iremos de caminata.*

We just climbed a volcano! *Subimos un volcán!*

I'm going to bring a walking stick. *Traeré un bastón.*

What a beautiful view! *Que linda vista.*

How far away is it? *Que tan lejos es?*

Sleeping Arrangements

We are all going to sleep in this room. *Todos dormiremos en este cuarto.*

How many people are sleeping here? *Cuántas personas están durmiendo aquí?*

Is it comfortable? *Es comodo?*

When do we wake up? *Cuando nos despertamos?*

What time do we go to sleep? *A qué hora nos dormimos?*

What time do you guys wake up? *Chicos a qué hora se levantan?*

Have you seen my backpack? *Han visto mi mochila?*

Are we going to sleep in sleeping bags? *Dormiremos en bolsas de dormir?*

Restroom Necessities

The toilet is stopped up with toilet paper, and I need to plunge it. *El inodoro está taqueado de papel y necesito destaquearlo.*

The bathroom is out of order. El baño está fuera de servicio.

I'm in here (the bathroom) so don't come in! *Estoy aquí en el cuarto de baño. No entren!*

Do you have any contact solution? *Tienes solución de contacto?*

I just need a roll of toilet paper. *Solo necesito un rollo de papel higiénico.*

I need to wash my hands. *Necesito lavar mis manos.*

I need a new pair underwear. *Necesito un nuevo par de ropa interior.*

I need an extra pair of socks. *Necesito un par de calcetines extras.*

The pipes are leaking. *Los tubos están goteando/filtrando.*

Out to Eat

I would like two slices of pepperoni pizza, please. *Quisiera dos rebanadas de pizza de pepperoni, por favor.*

I would like rice and beans. *Quisiera arroz y frijoles.*

Could you pass me the... *Puedes pasarme la...*

Can we sit in a booth instead of a table? *Nos podemos sentar en una cabina en vez de la mesa?*

Are you ready to eat? *Estás listo para comer?*

Are you pretty hungry? *Estás hambriento?/Estás con tigre?*

What's in it (the food)? *Que le echaron a la comida?*

No thank you, I'm full. *No gracias, estoy lleno./ No gracias, estoy satisfecho.*

I'm saving room for dessert/the other food. *Estoy guardando espacio para el postre/la otra comida.*

I need salt/pepper/spices. *Necesito sal/pimienta/chile.*

Church Talk

What religion are you? *De qué religión eres?*

Do you believe in God? *Crees en Dios?*

Are you a religious person? *Eres una persona religiosa?*

Is there a church near here? *Hay una iglesia cerca?*

When do you go to church? *Cuándo vas a la iglesia?*

Prayer Talk

Do you pray every day? *Oras todos los días?*

What do you pray about? *De qué oras?*

Would you like to pray with me? *Te gustaría orar conmigo?*

I feel blessed. *Me siento bendecido.*

Emergency

Be careful! *Cuidado!*

I've lost my...wallet. *Perdi mi... billetera.*

I can't find my...keys. *No encuentro mis ...llaves.*

I would like to report a theft. *Me gustaría informar de un robo.*

I've locked myself out of my room. *Me encerré fuera del cuarto.*

I am totally lost. *Estoy completamente perdido.*

Help! *Ayudame!*

Disaster Relief

We are bringing food and water. *Traemos comida y agua.*

Sand bags. *Bolsas de arena.*

We have a tent set up with supplies. *Tenemos una carta montada con suministros.*

Are you hurt? *Estás herido?*

Where are you hurt? *Dónde estás herido?*

Money Matters

I would like to change some money. *Me gustaría cambiar algo de dinero.*

Do you have any ID? *Tienes alguna identificación?*

Yes, I have my driver's license/passport.. *Si, tengo mi licencia de conducir/pasaporte.*

I have ___pesos/dollars.. *Tengo__pesos/corbobas.*

Personal Safety

God will watch over us and protect us. *Dios cuidará de nosotros y nos protegerá.*

Keep an eye out! *Mantén los ojos abiertos!*

Education

Where do you study? *Dónde estudias?*

Are you a student? *Eres estudiante?*

I'm going to take a gap year. *Tomaré un año sabático.*

What do you want to do once you've finished school? *Qué quieres hacer una vez que finalices la escuela?*

What do you want to study? *Qué quieres estudiar?*

Do you like to learn about new things? *Te gusta aprender sobre nuevas cosas?*

I have been learning a lot of Spanish over the past month. *He estado aprendiendo mucho español en el último mes.*

I really only started learning Spanish seriously about a month ago. *En realidad, sólo empecé a aprender español en serio hace aproximadamente un mes.*

I have been learning by reading articles, watching movies, listening to music, and memorizing important words and phrases. *He estado aprendiendo por la lectura de artículos, ver películas, escuchar música, y memorizar palabras y frases importantes.*

Forgive me if there are some words that I don't understand. *Perdóname si hay algunas palabras que no entiendo.*

I still have not mastered Spanish. *Todavía no domino el español.*

What grade are you in? *En qué grado estás?*

I am a student studying….(your major). *Soy estudiante estudiando...*

I am in high school. *Estoy en secundaria.*

Do you want to read a book with me? *Te gustaría leer un libro conmigo?*

Meeting New Friends

What do you do for fun? *Qué haces para divertirte?*

What do you do for work? *En qué trabajas?*

I read a lot about… *Leo mucho sobre...*

I am really interested in languages, history, cultures and religions. *Estoy muy interesado en las lenguas, culturas y religiones.*

Have you watched any good movies? *Has mirado algunas buenas películas?*

What kind of music do you like? *Qué tipo de musica te gusta?*

What line of work are you in? *En qué línea de trabajo te encuentras?*

I just started working at a new job. *Acabo de empezar a trabajar en nuevo trabajo.*

I'm doing an internship. *Estoy haciendo una pasantía.*

I'm retired, and now I'm here to help out my fellow man. *Estoy jubilado, y ahora estoy aquí para ayudar a mi prójimo.*

Do you want to come with us to the town? *Quieres venir con nosotros al centro?*

Let me know if you can make it! *Avísame si puedes venir!*

What time should we meet up? *A qué hora debemos encontrarnos?*

Do you have any plans for tomorrow morning/afternoon? *Tienes algún plan para mañana por la mañana o por la tarde?*

Are you free to hang out later? *Estás libre para pasar más tarde?*

What have you been up to? *Qué has estado haciendo?*

What is your name? *Cuál es tu nombre? Cómo te llamas?*

Nice to meet you. *Un gusto conocerte./Mucho gusto.*

We are going to visit to a retirement home! *Visitaremos una casa de retiro.*

Thank you for your hospitality. *Gracias por tu hospitalidad.*

This is my friend. He doesn't speak Spanish. *Este es mi amigo. Él no habla español.*

Ministry

Would you like to come to church with us? *Te gustarías venir a la iglesia con nosotros?*

Do you go to church often? *Vas a la iglesia a menudo?*

We are going to have an event today, would you like to come? *Tendremos un evento hoy, te gustaría venir?*

We will have music and praise and worship. *Tendremos música, alabanza y adoración.*

We are all getting together to praise the Lord. *Todos nos estamos reuniendo para alabar al Señor.*

Would you like to stop by for a little while? *Te gustaría venir por poco tiempo?*

We will be having dinner just before the event. *Tendremos la cena antes del evento.*

At the Market

What should I buy while I'm at the market? *Que debo comprar mientras estoy en el mercado?*

Could you tell me where the___is? Podrías *decirme dónde está el/la _____.*

Do you accept credit or debit cards? *Aceptas tarjetas de crédito o de débito?*

How much does it cost? *Cuánto cuesta/Cuánto vale?*

I don't have that much (money). *No tengo ese dinero.*

How much are you going to charge me? *Cuánto me cobrarás?*

It's fine. Keep the change. Thanks. *Está bien, quédate con el cambio. Gracias.*

Where is the candy isle? *Dónde está la isla de caramelos/confites?*

Saying Goodbye (For Now)

Thank you for your hospitality! *Gracias por tu hospitalidad!*

We will see each other again! *Nos veremos otra vez!*

Take care of yourself! *Cuídate!*

I am so happy to have met you. *Estoy feliz de haberte conocido.*

Thank you for being so kind over these past few days. *Gracias por ser tan amable en estos días.*

I hope to return very soon. *Espero volver muy pronto.*

Don't worry, we will be back! *No te preocupes, volveremos!*

I told myself I wouldn't cry. *Me dije a mi mismo no lloraré.*

Goodbye, for now! *Adios por ahora!*

When do you leave? *Cuando te vás?*

We leave this weekend. *Salimos este fin de semana.*

Miscellaneous

Are you allergic to grapefruit? *Eres alérgico a la toronja?*

The day after tomorrow. *Pasado mañana.*

What time is it? *Qué hora es?*

I ripped my pants. *Dañé mis pantalones.*

I have a journal to write about my time here. *Tengo un diario para escribir sobre mi tiempo aquí.*

Snake. *Serpiente/ Culebra.*

Chapter 10: Bringing It All Together

This is it. We have reached the end of the book, but the beginning of your mission trip! Take a moment to look back on all that you have accomplished. No doubt you took some of the phrases here and added them to your list, but I am confident that you also learned some important words from your language partner, your movies, your articles, and the YouTubers that helped you.

As you can probably tell, this book has given you the tools to succeed. Nowhere did you hear me talk about getting a Spanish-speaking love interest, putting sticky notes all over your room, or asking your Spanish-speaking friends to talk to you in Spanish as much as possible. By now, you know why that is. It's because those methods are easy for people to say, easy for online articles to promote, but they are so out of touch with what it really takes to become proficient in a language. Luckily, you took the more intelligent approach. You took the time to get to know the language and the people who speak it, and you have prepared yourself well for your mission trip to Latin America.

So go on now. Go and do good things in the world. Work to make the lives of those you serve better.

While you are over there, might I suggest one last thing?

Keep a journal of your time out of the country. I remember when I first left home to visit a foreign country. I went to the heart of Mexico (Guanajuato) two days after I graduated from high school. I made sure that I took notes in a small notebook after each day was over, and made sure to write in all the new Spanish words that I was learning. I encourage you to do the same, to keep a journal. You will find that this little gem will stay with you for the rest of your life and will provide you with extra encouragement to get back out there and to be the light of Christ in the world.

Oh and one last thing (for real this time). If you found this book to be helpful, there is only one thing that I ask. Please write a review of the book on Amazon. It would mean a lot to me and would help me out a great deal!

Remember that here at Mission Trip Spanish, the goal is to give you the plain honest truth about how you can learn the Spanish you need for your mission trip. But this book is only the beginning!

Learn more about what we are doing here at Mission Trip Spanish, read our blog posts, and get updates on new books and content at www.MissionTripSpanish.com

Sign up for the email list, and I will send you updates. I'll even let you know when to look for new books on Amazon before they launch!

Thanks for reading.

Your Friend,

Tyler

[1]Gleason, Jean Berko, and Nan Bernstein Ratner. "The development of language." (2005).

[2]Winke, Paula M. "The psychology of the language learner: Individual differences in second language acquisition." *Studies in Second Language Acquisition* 29.01 (2007): 143-144. The "individual differences (IDs) in SLA presents research on topics such as language aptitude, motivation, cognitive styles, student self-regulation, and personality traits." There are many disciplines under each of these second language acquisition categories.

[3]Piske, Thorsten, Ian RA MacKay, and James E. Flege. "Factors affecting degree of foreign accent in an L2: A review." *Journal of phonetics* 29.2 (2001): 191-215. "As expected from the literature review, both age of L2 [Language 2] learning and amount of continued L1 [Language 1] use were found to affect degree of foreign accent. Gender, length of residence in an L2-speaking country and self-estimated L1 ability, on the other hand, were not found to have a significant, independent effect on overall L2 pronunciation accuracy."

[4]Nelson, Ardis L., and Jessica L. Scott. "Applied Spanish in the university curriculum: A successful model for community-based service-learning."*Hispania* (2008): 446-460. "...**Textbook Spanish**, written by very educated people, is completely different"

[5]Thorne, Steven L., Rebecca W. Black, and Julie M. Sykes. "Second language use, socialization, and learning in Internet interest communities and online gaming." *The Modern Language Journal* 93.s1 (2009): 802-821.

[6]Krashen, Stephen. "The case for narrow reading." *Language Magazine* 3.5 (2004): 17-19.c

[7]Gold, Sunny Sea. "How to Be a Better Time Manager." *Scientific American Mind* 25.5 (2014): 14-14.

Made in United States
Orlando, FL
14 July 2025

62936770R00042